KEIKO ABE

安倍圭子　マリンバ二重奏曲集

Works for Marimba Duo

SCHOTT

SJ-052

CONTENTS   ●   目次

Memories of the Seashore II

遙かな海 II

Keiko Abe
安倍圭子

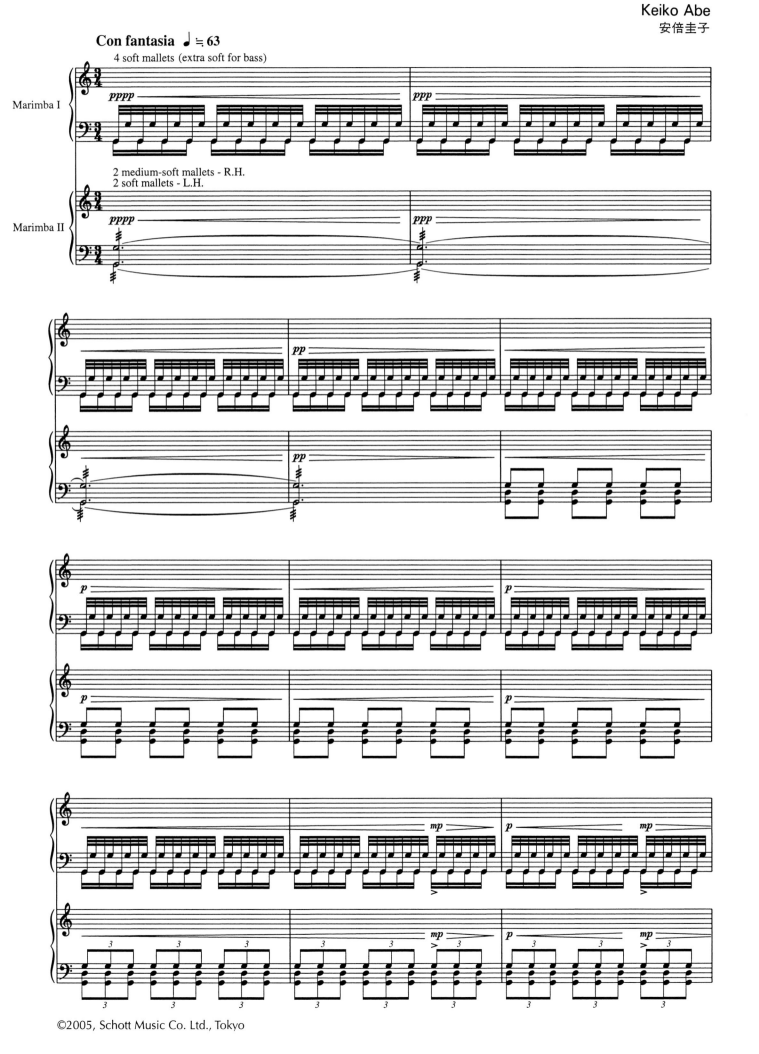

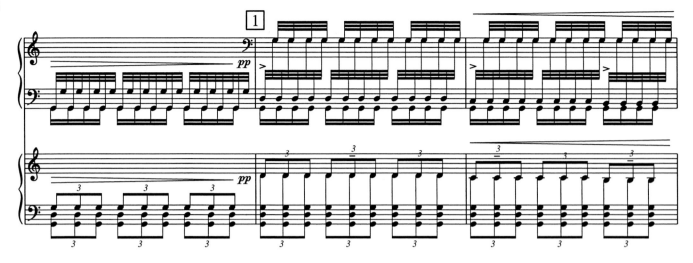

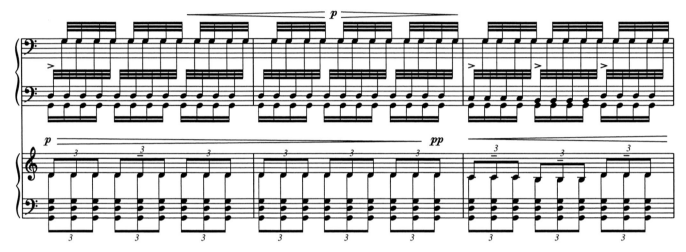

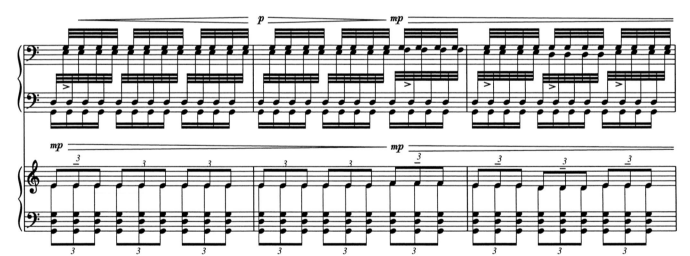

poco a poco cresc.

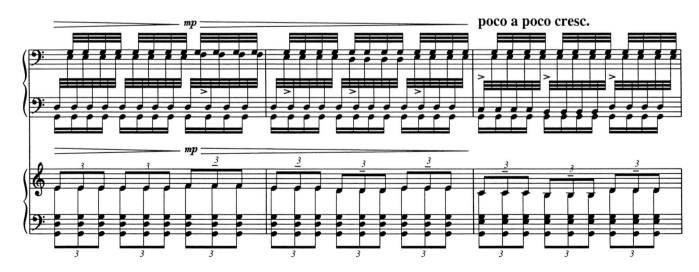

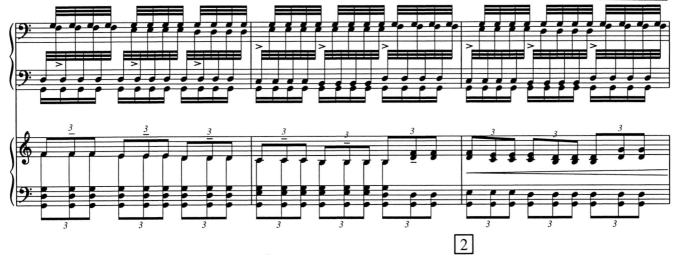

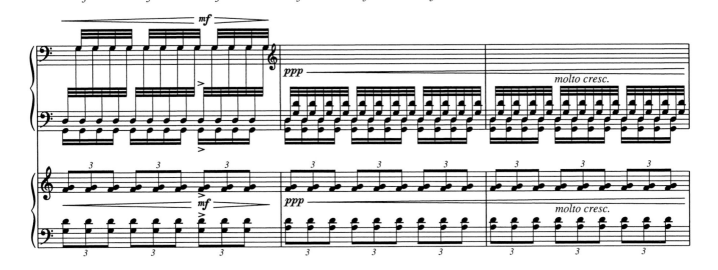

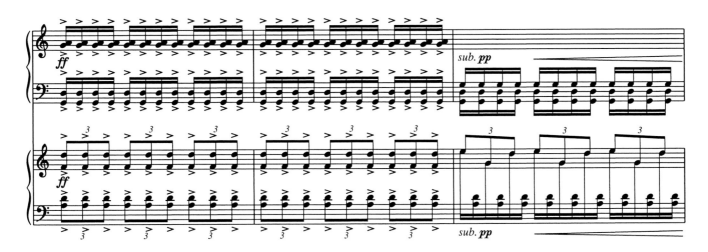

6

poco a poco rit. e dim.

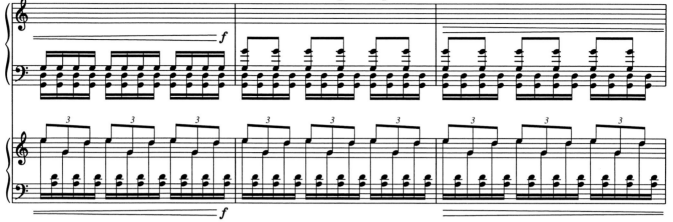

Cantabile
3 ♩ = 60

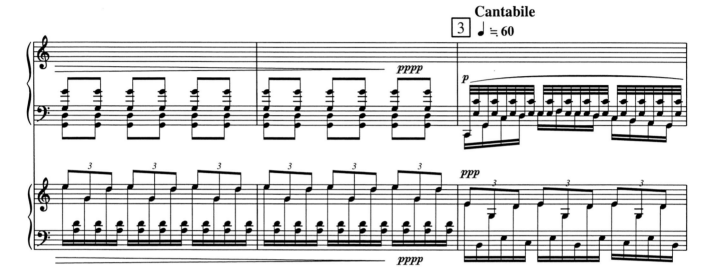

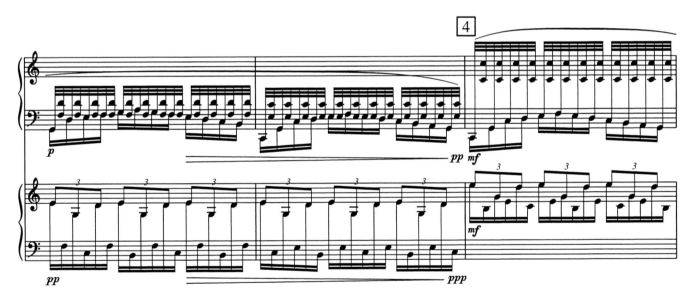

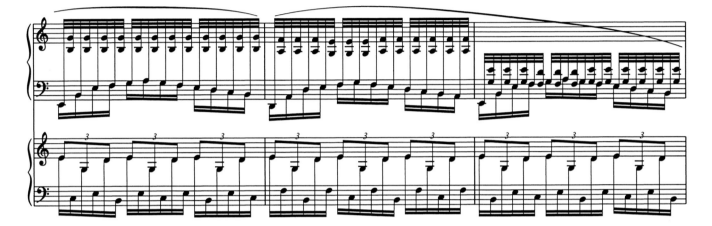

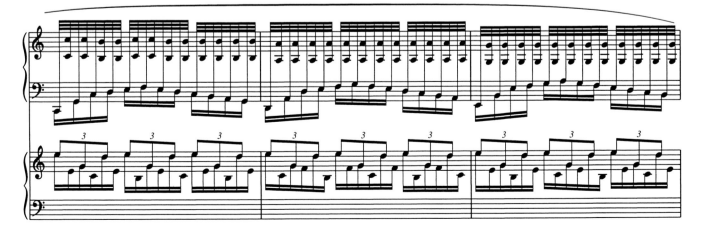

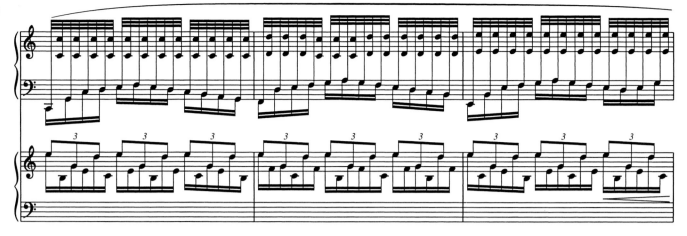

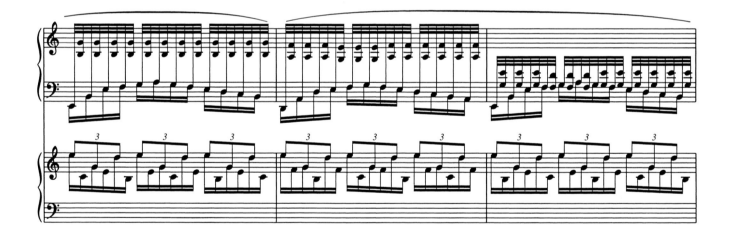

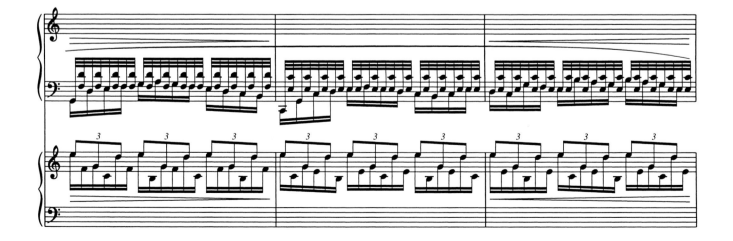

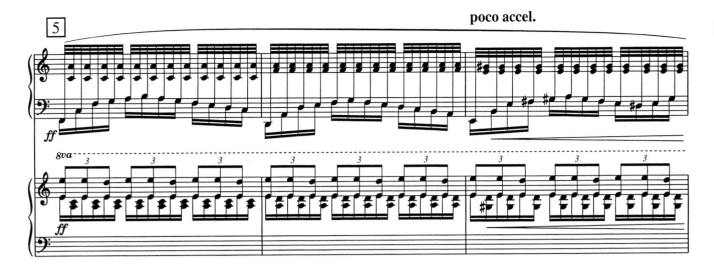

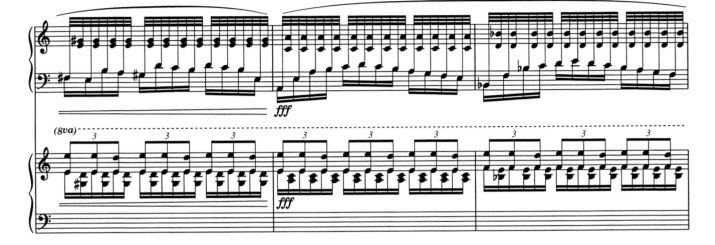

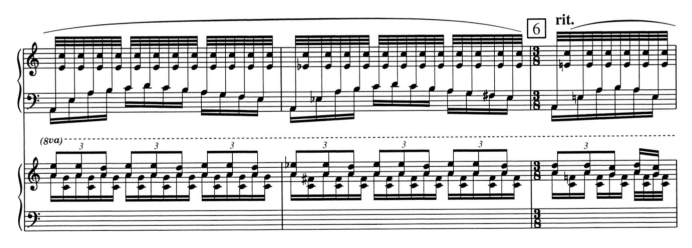

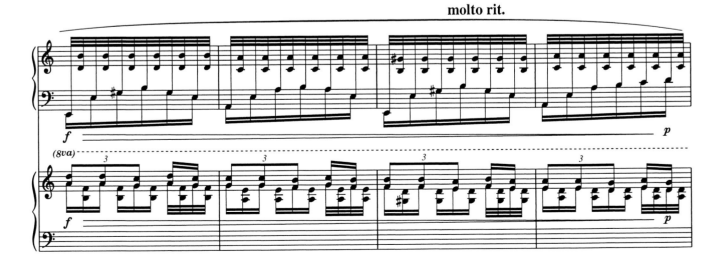

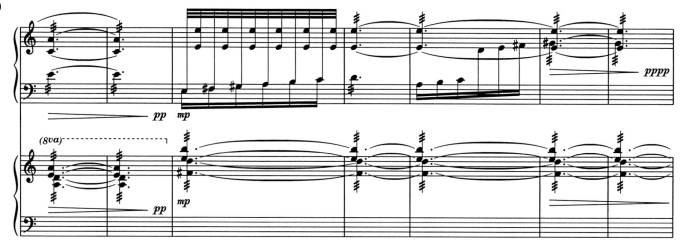

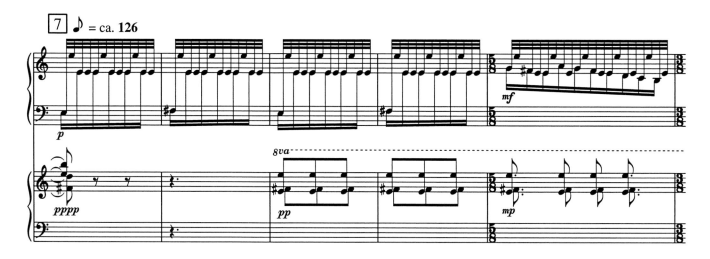

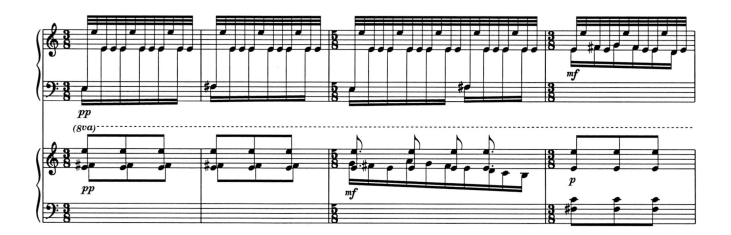

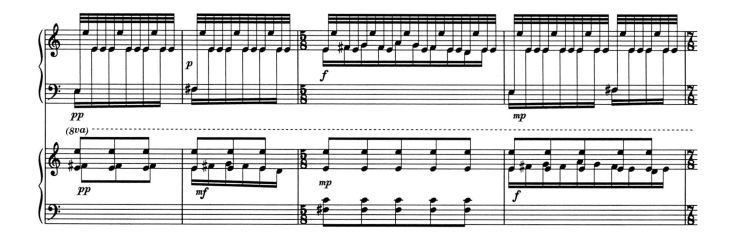

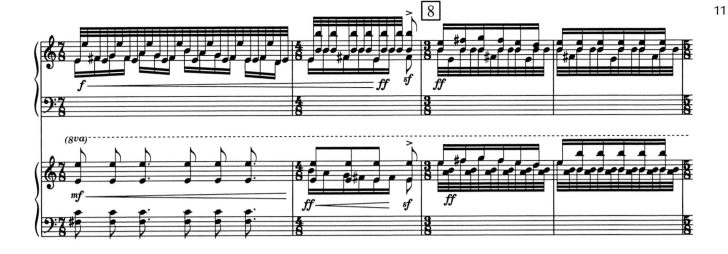

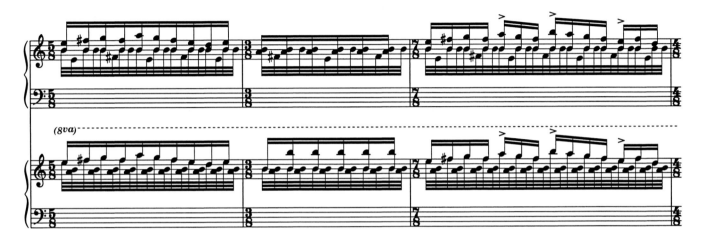

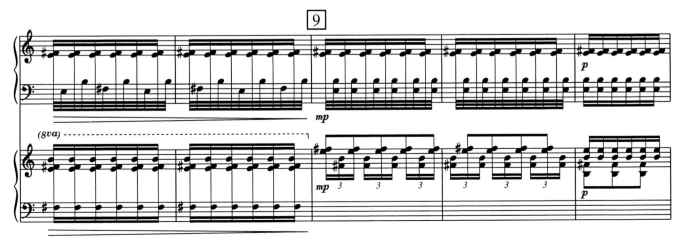

12

poco a poco rit.

rit.

Tranquillo
10 ♩ ≒ 60

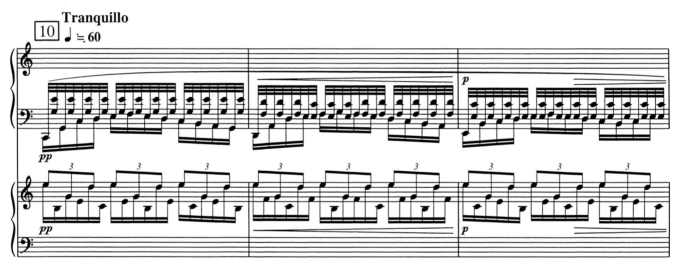

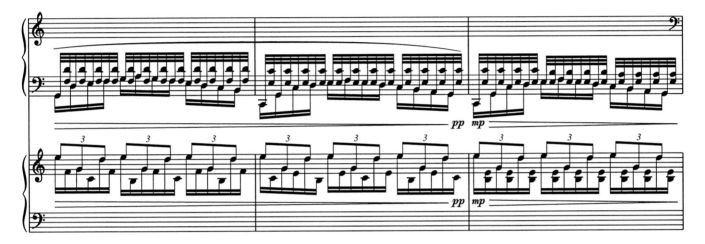

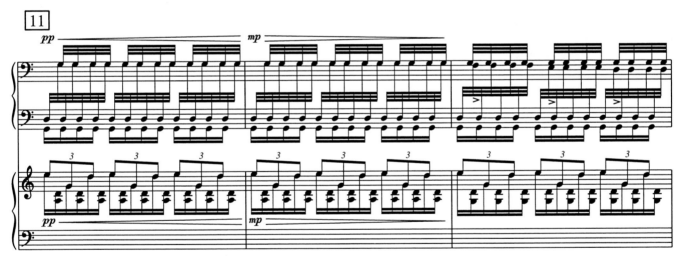

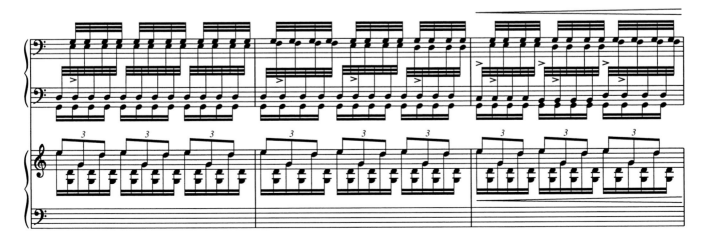

12

poco a poco rit. e dim.

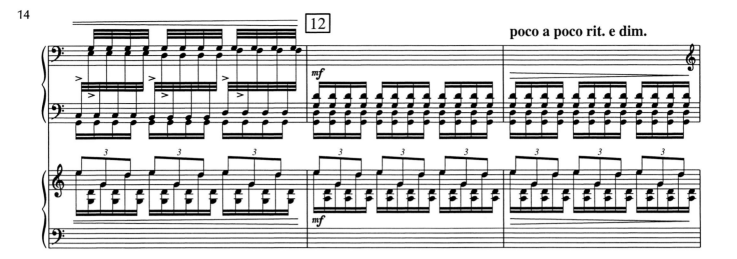

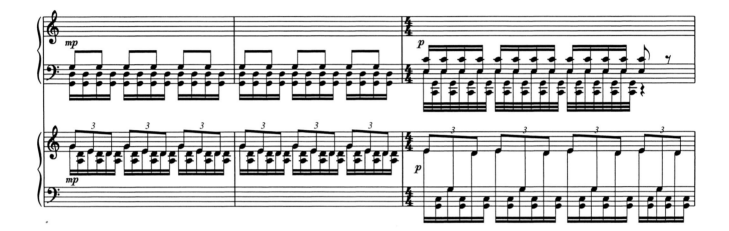

molto rit.

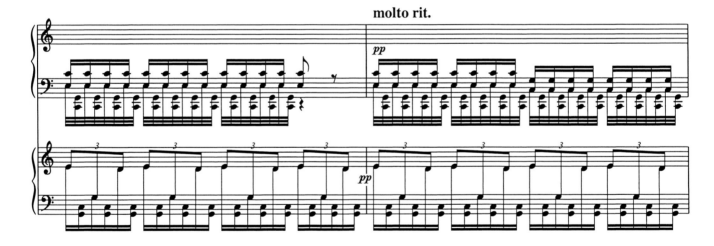

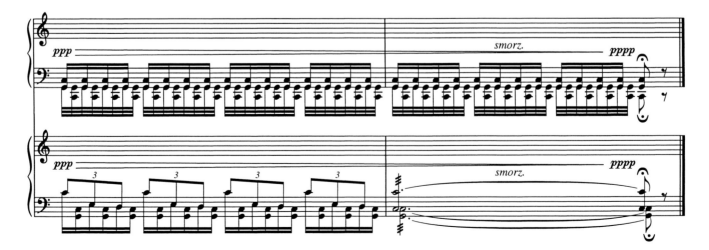

Wind in the Bamboo Grove II

竹林 II

Keiko Abe
安倍圭子

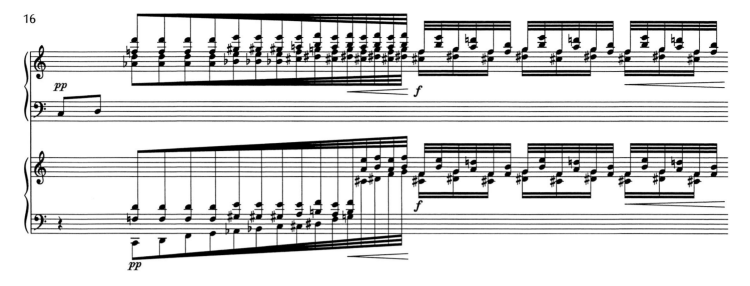

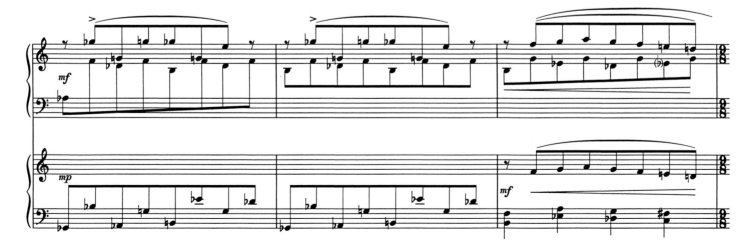

poco a poco rit.

✳ = Strike edge of bar with handle of mallet.
音板の端をマレットの柄の部分で打つ。

Cadenza

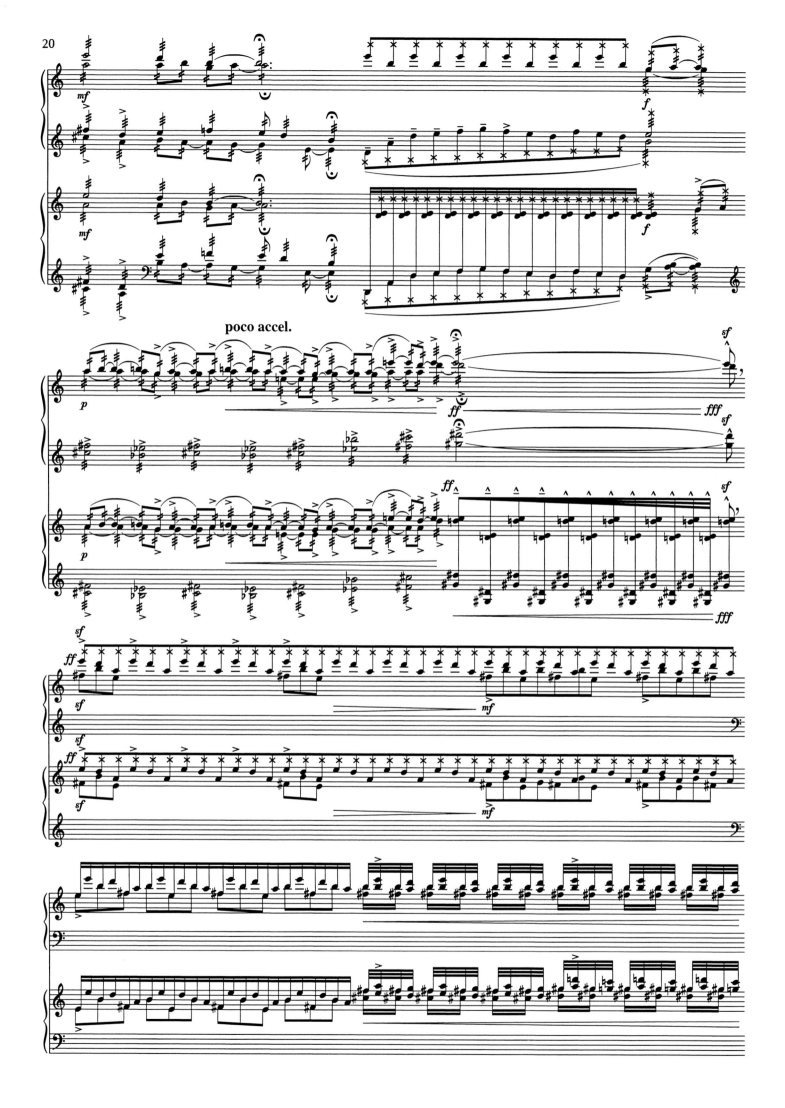

poco accel.

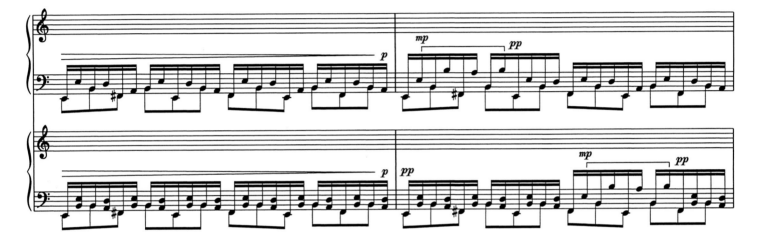

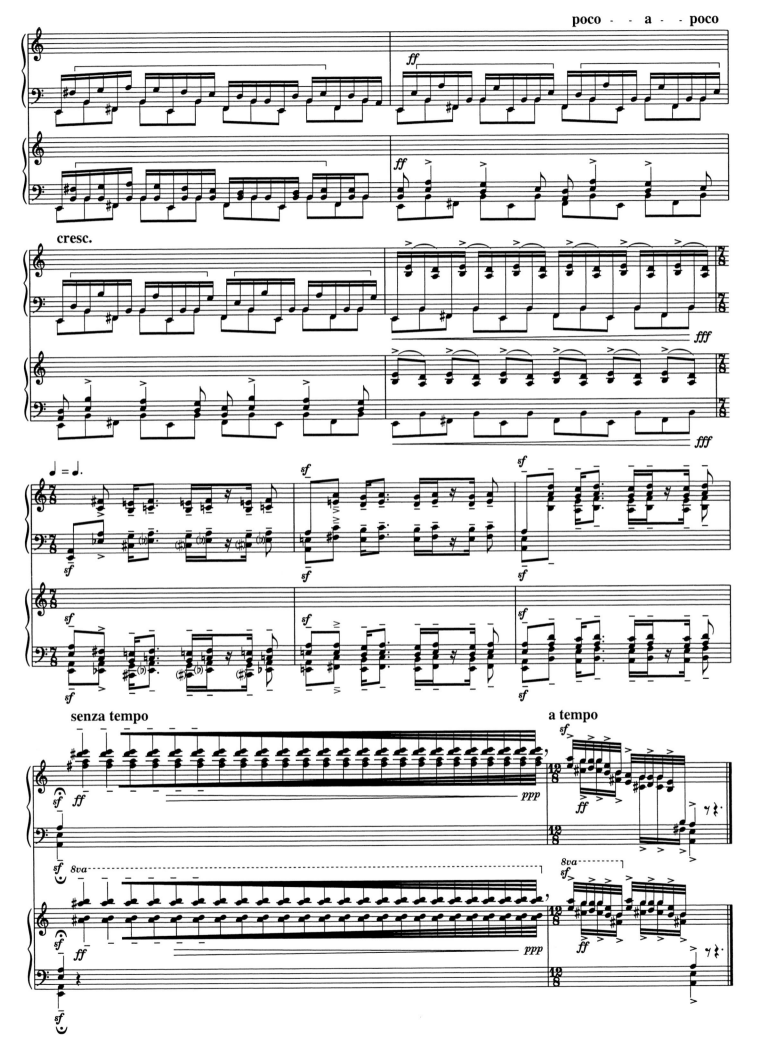

安倍圭子《マリンバ二重奏曲集》　　　　●

初版発行————————————————2005年5月25日

第1版第3刷③————————————2018年8月10日

発行————————————————ショット・ミュージック株式会社

　　　　　　　　　　　　　　　　　　　　　東京都千代田区内神田1-10-1 平富ビル3階

　　　　　　　　　　　　　　　　　　　　　〒101-0047

　　　　　　　　　　　　　　　　　　　　　(03)6695-2450

　　　　　　　　　　　　　　　　　　　　　http://www.schottjapan.com

　　　　　　　　　　　　　　　　　　　　　ISBN 978-4-89066-052-0

　　　　　　　　　　　　　　　　　　　　　ISMN M-65001-206-5